Psalms for
WOMEN

PRESENTED TO:

_____

PRESENTED BY:

_____

DATE:

_____

Psalms for WOMEN

GOD'S GIFT
OF JOY
AND ENCOURAGEMENT

HONOR
BOOKS

Tulsa, Oklahoma

This is My resting place forever;

Here I will dwell, for I have desired it.

I will abundantly bless her provision;

I will satisfy her poor with bread.

PSALM 132:14 NKJV

God's Provision and Abundance in Our Lives

But all who humble themselves before the Lord
shall be given every blessing,
and shall have wonderful peace.

PSALM 37:11 TLB

It would be a special moment in any woman's life. She has
prepared a wonderful dinner for her loved ones and friends. The dining
room table is set with her best china and silver. A lovely centerpiece
graces the table. Late afternoon light streams in
the window and glints merrily off the crystal
goblets. As she takes in the festive scene
around her, she can almost hear the happy,
laughing voices that will soon fill the
room.

Her heart swells with gladness and
thanks. The table and meal she has
prepared have triggered a reverie about the
many blessings she has received in life, none
more dear to her than the company of her
family and treasured friends. The evening will
become a fond memory, she knows, and contribute to the legacy she is
building for her family.

Thank You, Lord, for the bounty and fullness in my life. You make all
good things possible and repay my devotion and loyalty to Your
commandments with unimaginable kindnesses.

May God be gracious to us and bless us
and make his face to shine upon us,
that your way may be known upon earth,
your saving power among all nations.
Let the peoples praise you, O God;
let all the peoples praise you.

PSALM 67:1-3 NRSV

God's Help in Times of Need

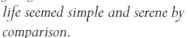

The salvation of the righteous is from the LORD;
he is their refuge in the time of trouble.
PSALM 37:39 NRSV

Today's woman can attest to the squeeze she feels, caught in the middle with pressing demands on every side. Truly she is part of the "sandwich generation." With a husband and children to care for, older parents to attend, a home to look after, and, usually, a career that keeps her racing to keep up, she often feels overwhelmed. Her mother's life seemed simple and serene by comparison.

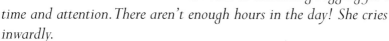

She tries to remember that these obligations also carry many opportunities for blessing— opportunities to develop individual talents, contribute to household income, and enjoy the mature company of her parents, who are likely to live longer than earlier generations. And yet everywhere she looks, she sees someone or something begging for her time and attention. There aren't enough hours in the day! She cries inwardly.

Lord, when I feel like I am juggling an impossible number of priorities and guilt threatens to crush me, come to my aid with Your amazing grace. Preserve and strengthen me and those I love.

Nothing bad will happen to you;
no disaster will come to your home.
He has put his angels in charge of you
to watch over you wherever you go.

PSALM 91:10-11 NCV

God's Protection

God is our refuge and strength,
a very present help in trouble.

PSALM 46:1 NRSV

A mother's concern for her children knows no bounds. Their welfare is foremost in everything she does. Secure in their mother's love, children grow into healthy, well-adjusted adults. They approach life's challenges with confidence and poise. They are equipped to achieve great things. When crises arise, they draw on the strength of the unconditional love their mother provides for them.

In the same way, God pours out His love and concern on us. And as His children, we learn to trust and rely upon Him. Over time and through experience, we learn that we can abandon ourselves to His care. Daily, on more than one occasion, we turn to Him, like children to their mothers. And when we do, He is always there to meet us. His constant protection allows us to grow strong and confident, and enables us to accomplish great things in His name.

*L*ord, help me every morning, to turn my day over to You. Teach me to put all my plans and all my fears in Your hands. I know that Your constant love will always be there to protect me.

But as for me, I will come into your Temple
protected by your mercy and your love;
I will worship you with deepest awe.

PSALM 5:7 TLB

Our Thankfulness and Praise to God

Clap your hands, all you peoples;
shout to God with loud songs of joy.
For the LORD, the Most High, is awesome,
a great king over all the earth.

PSALM 47:1-2 NRSV

*H*ow often we forget to be grateful, letting daily worries distract us from the abundance that is ours. Mortgage payments, troublesome children, a headache, even a burned pizza can interfere with our appreciation for the blessings we have been given.

We should open all our prayers with the praise and thanksgiving that are God's due. When we wake in the morning and before we fall asleep at night, praise and thanksgiving should be our first and last thoughts. For whatever our circumstances may be, God has in fact given us the gift of life in the here and now and the promise of life everlasting in the future.

*L*ord, help me always remember that I am Your child and the endowment You have given me is beyond reckoning. I am rich in love and comfort, and my heart is full to the brim. I praise You and thank You for all You have given me.

Your great love reaches to the skies,
your truth to the heavens.
God, you are supreme above the skies.
Let your glory be over all the earth.

PSALM 108:4-5 NCV

God's Faithfulness

All those who know your mercy, Lord,
will count on you for help.
For you have never yet forsaken those who trust in you.

PSALM 9:10 TLB

*T*he vows and promises we exchange with those we love provide us with a strong foundation on which to build our lives. The faithfulness we both give and receive fills us with confidence and comforts us in our times of need. But the faithfulness of our closest family and friends appears as a pale shadow next to the splendor of God's faithfulness.

God is faithful to us no matter what. He gives us His full attention when we reach out for His love, assurance, and support. God never breaks His promises. And He is always there for us. By believing this and affirming it often, we take on a measure of His strength and reflect His goodness to others.

*L*ord, let me walk this earth with the confidence that You are my God. And help me always to trust in Your faithful love, guidance, and protection.

But I am like an olive tree
growing in God's house,
and I can count on his love
forever and ever.

PSALM 52:8 CEV

Cast your burden on the LORD,
and he will sustain you;
he will never permit
the righteous to be moved.

PSALM 55:22 NRSV

Our Seeking and Yearning for God

Hear my cry, O God;
listen to my prayer.
From the end of the earth I call to you,
when my heart is faint.

PSALM 61:1-2 NRSV

Until we place our lives fully in His hands, we will never quiet the anxious thoughts that cry out from within and leave us feeling unhappy and defeated. We search frantically for happiness, success, and fulfillment. We flail about and wonder why we are never satisfied, why we are always restless. We wonder why new acquisitions merely whet our desire for more.

What we are yearning for—and so artlessly trying to find—has been there all the time. God alone can satisfy our desperate longings. Without Him, even the sources of human happiness, such as children, family, homes, fond possessions, dreams, and ambitions, invite stress and agitation because we know one day we will lose them. Only when we make God the center of our lives will we find true fulfillment.

Lord, as I look to You, fill my life to overflowing with Your peace and joy. Keep me always in the palm of Your hand.

Shew me thy ways, O Lord; teach me thy paths.
Lead me in thy truth, and teach me:
for thou art the God of my salvation;
on thee do I wait all the day.

PSALM 25: 4-5 KJV

God's Joy and Delight in Our Lives

The LORD is kind and shows mercy.
He does not become angry quickly but is full of love.
The LORD is good to everyone;
he is merciful to all he has made.

PSALM 145: 8-9 NCV

When we think of those we love—family and friends, mentors and heroes—joy and affection fill our hearts. Because they are in the world, our lives are brighter and more meaningful. We watch for

opportunities to show them how much we care for them and value them. We jump at chances to nourish and sustain them, to cheer them and make their hearts glad. Their very existence is a cause for celebration. When they are happy, we are happy.

As children of God, we mimic Him in these feelings for our loved ones, feelings that are dim reflections of His profound delight in us as His children. He wants to see us happy and fulfilled, and He wants us to know He is the Source of the abundant blessings in our lives.

Lord, knowing that I am Your child brings me great joy and delight. Help me follow Your commandments, and please guard my relationship with You so I might achieve with happiness all that I was created to do.

You protected me from death
and kept me from stumbling,
so that I would please you
and follow the light that leads to life.

PSALM 56:13 CEV

God's Direction and Correction

I will instruct thee and teach thee in the way
which thou shalt go:
I will guide thee with mine eye.
PSALM 32:8 KJV

*M*arried couples often develop a shorthand style of communication over time. A gesture, a raised eyebrow, a certain cough or pause between words can speak volumes and quickly convey to one

exactly where the other stands concerning a certain issue or situation. They become so attuned to each other's strengths, weaknesses, quirks, and foibles that they can almost predict what the other will do or say.

In much the same way, it is possible to establish such a close and satisfying relationship with God that we gain new confidence in our ability to receive direction and correction from Him. As we bask in His love and give careful attention to His will, we become familiar with His ways. We feel keenly His approval or disapproval and can see His hand at work in our lives.

*L*ord, help me take stock every day of what You are doing in my life and where You are leading me. I truly want to know You better.

The steps of the godly are directed by the LORD.
He delights in every detail of their lives.
Though they stumble, they will not fall,
for the LORD holds them by the hand.

PSALM 37:23-24 NLT

Our Comfort in God

I have set the L<small>ORD</small> always before me:
because he is at my right hand, I shall not be moved.
PSALM **16:8** KJV

We live with a daily onslaught of tragic news from around the world and close to home—sad images from the television, heartbreaking stories from a dear friend. These hard realities can rob us of our joy and replace it with fear.

We must constantly bolster our hope in the eternal love and protection of God, who guides us always through the power of the Holy Spirit. His power touches our hearts, minds, and souls. This mystery of the Lord's daily work in our lives is beyond our ability to understand. It is the great mystery of life that we are, as children of God,

tabernacles of His Holy Spirit and, thus, mighty and invincible with Him and through Him. Our fears can be laid to rest. We need only acknowledge His presence and take Him at His word, giving Him our cares and burdens and placing our trust completely in Him.

Lord, all I have and all I am comes from You. I place myself wholly in Your will and know You will care for me and quiet my fears.

The LORD will give strength unto his people;
the LORD will bless his people with peace.

PSALM 29:11 KJV

I sleep and wake up refreshed,
because you, LORD,
protect me.

PSALM 3:5 CEV

Loving God

I love you, LORD; you are my strength.

PSALM 18:1 NLT

*G*od's grandeur inspires awe. His perfect goodness is imponderable. He is so big; we are so small. He is beyond our understanding. How then can we love Him? By making Him part of our daily lives and embracing Him as our Father.

To do that, we must first acknowledge our utter dependence on Him. We must gaze at the world around us with new eyes, eyes full of love and admiration for His countless wonders. We must constantly remind ourselves that His handiwork is everywhere and in everything, and that He is greater than the most marvelous thing we can imagine. We must wake up to the truth that we are important because He made us, He loves us, He protects us, and He preserves us.

*L*ord, help me wake up each morning with a hallelujah in my heart. Help me share all my confidences with You, and express all my fears to You. Help me keep Your commandments. And help me end each day by whispering an amen to You as I go to sleep.

Let all those who seek You
rejoice and be glad in You:
Let such as love Your salvation say continually,
"The LORD be magnified!"

PSALM 40:16 NKJV

God's Mercy and Compassion

The LORD is kind and does what is right;
our God is merciful.

PSALM 116:5 NCV

*G*od's mercy and compassion make life bearable and invest it with meaning. We pray to Him for aid, and He answers us! We ask Him, the Lord of light, to protect us, and He does just that. We implore Him for wisdom and guidance, and He gives it freely. His deep and abiding concern for us, as His children, is manifest in the steadfast love He shows us.

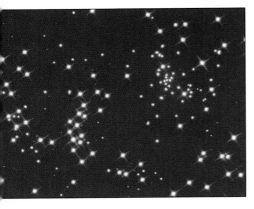

How comforting it is to rest in God's mercy—to know beyond a shadow of a doubt that no matter where we fail, no matter what we might fear, His mercy abounds. It never ends. It is infinite. How reassuring it is to know that He feels compassion for us and intervenes in our everyday lives with the blessings of His divine mercy.

*L*ord, thank You for Your mercy that is poured out on me. I depend upon it each and every day. Give me a merciful and compassionate heart like Yours. And teach me to reach out to others as You have reached out to me.

The LORD is like a father to his children,
tender and compassionate to those who fear him.

PSALM 103:13 NLT

Say "thank you" to the Lord for being so good,
for always being so loving and kind.

PSALM 107:1 TLB

God's Power, Presence, and Peace

He will give his people strength.
He will bless them with peace.

PSALM 29:11 TLB

*W*e all have moments in which we sense God's power, presence, and peace—moments when the clouds part and a sudden, all-prevailing sense of peace washes over us. We know then that we are truly loved by Almighty God, and we are filled with gratitude and a new sense of security. It is as if we have suddenly discovered who we really are, and we feel more alive than ever.

These moments become more frequent if we cultivate quality time with Him. This requires spiritual discipline and fortitude. If we determine to pursue this course, however, the rewards are boundless and our lives will be immeasurably enriched. Daily prayer, Scripture reading, and meditation on God's attributes will deepen our understanding and make us ready receptacles for His grace.

*L*ord, I don't want to wait until I get to heaven to enjoy Your power, Your presence, and Your peace. Help me receive all that You have for me each and every day.

The LORD's voice is heard over the sea.
The glorious God thunders;
the LORD thunders over the ocean.

PSALM 29:3 NCV

God's Greatness and Majesty

My whole being, praise the LORD.
LORD my God, you are very great.

PSALM 104:1 NCV

---

*T*he best way to appreciate the grandeur and glory of God is to shed our weariness and worldly wisdom and begin to see things through childlike eyes. Doing so returns to us our sense of wonder and

awe. Christ said as much when he encouraged us to become as little children, awed by life, but trusting nonetheless in our Father.

God's greatness and majesty are evidenced

everywhere if we look at the world with childlike eyes—birds fly from branch to branch, fish swim in the sea, stars shoot across the night sky. And children do not have difficulty believing that God made all these things, that He created each and every one.

---

*L*ord, help me never to become so grown up that I no longer revel in the glory of Your creation or accept Your unconditional love for me.

I will praise thee;
for I am fearfully and wonderfully made:
Marvelous are thy works;
and that my soul knoweth right well.

PSALM 139:14 KJV

God's Love for Us

As for the godly people in the world,
they are the wonderful ones I enjoy.

PSALM 16:3 NCV

God's love for us is so immense and absolute that it is really impossible for us to comprehend. The nearest we can come to understanding His love is to compare it to our love for our children. The mother-child relationship is one of the most intimate and caring of all human relationships. A mother's greatest delight is to see her child happy and prospering. Her greatest fears are those for her child. A mother's love is unconditional. There is nothing her child can do that she will not forgive. There is nothing she will not do to protect her child, even if it means losing her own life.

Yet God's love is even greater than a mother's love. It is greater than any human love we can ever know. And our only possible response is to open our hearts and receive this incomprehensible blessing.

Lord, open my heart to receive Your love and selfless concern for me. And teach me to let that love flow out to those around me, that they also may be blessed.

He loveth righteousness and judgment:
the earth is full of the goodness of the LORD.

PSALM 33:5 KJV

God Listens to Our Prayers

Through each night I sing his songs,
praying to God who gives me life.

PSALM 42:8 NLT

*P*ulled between the demands of work and family, we have little opportunity for quiet time. The moments when we can experience God without distraction and interruption are few and precious. The faces of our loved ones are never far from our minds, reminding, cajoling, requesting. And the responsibilities of home and career follow us wherever we go.

Yet no matter how fragmented and abbreviated our prayers may become, we can be sure God hears them—not only in those rare moments of peace but also during the frantic hours of activity. He hears us loud and clear, no matter how mumbled and inarticulate our message may seem. And He is quick to give us the right words to say, the proper response to a crisis, and the kindness and diplomacy we need to navigate our complex and difficult days.

*L*ord, I bring all my cares to You. Thank You for listening and answering me. And thank You for keeping Your mighty hand on my life, guiding and comforting me through my days here on earth.

O Lord, hear me praying;
listen to my plea, O God my King,
for I will never pray to anyone but you.

PSALM 5:1 TLB

Prayer Banishes Worry and Fear

Hear my voice, O God, in my meditation;
Preserve my life from fear of the enemy.
PSALM 64:1 NKJV

Worry and fear are the bane of human existence. They cripple and incapacitate us. And they strike when we feel far from God. They rise up and crash over us when we are not paying attention to what is really important in life—our relationship with God. The more we pray, the closer we draw to God and the better we know Him. And the more we pray, the more His presence and power surround us, lifting us up and dissolving our worries and fears. We can cope with whatever comes along because we know we are shored up and strengthened with what He has promised us. We have become recipients of His bountiful grace.

Lord, I know that You will supply all my needs as I am faithful to trust You and walk with You in prayer. Cause faith to rise up in my heart as I look to You for all that I need.

I cry out to God Most High,
to the God who does everything for me.
He sends help from heaven and saves me.
He punishes those who chase me.
God sends me his love and truth.

PSALM 57:2-3 NCV

God Lightens Our Cares and Burdens

Commit everything you do to the Lord.
Trust him to help you do it and he will.

PSALM 37:5 TLB

Many women find that keeping a journal is an enhancement to their spiritual lives. They may not write in it every day, but they do write often enough to record those things that are uppermost on their minds. The act of writing down our worries and cares is liberating and exhilarating, for we are forced to examine and articulate the sources of our anxiety. When these are identified and analyzed and ultimately committed to God, they lose their power over us.

Journaling our worries to God is an effective discipline for reducing stress. In a way, it is like writing God a letter and asking Him to take care of things. Once we have done so, we can close our journals, put up our pens, and go about the day relieved and refreshed that our troubles have been dealt with effectively.

Lord, as I write down my concerns, I release them into Your capable arms. Thank You for caring for me so much that You are concerned with each entry no matter how great or small it might be.

I praise God for his word.
I trust God, so I am not afraid.

Psalm 56:4 NCV

Prayer Helps Us Make Decisions

With my whole heart have I sought thee:
O let me not wander from thy commandments.

PSALM 119:10 KJV

*T*hroughout our lives, we are presented with choices. And those choices are not often simple issues of right and wrong. Indeed the most

difficult situations we face have to do with choosing from a variety of possibilities, with varying shades of good and bad.

Fortunately, we do not have to deal with difficult choices alone and unaided. If we ask God, He will enlighten us. He will show us the way to go. He has already given us His commandments to light our way through the maze of facts and emotions. And He waits patiently for us to bring each one before Him. He is eager to help us do what is right for our lives and the lives of those we love.

*L*ord, thank You for listening as I bring my decisions before You. Thank You for the direction You give and the way You fill my heart with quiet assurance.

Thy word have I hid in mine heart,
that I might not sin against thee.

PSALM 119:11 KJV

I love the Lord because he hears my prayers
and answers them.

PSALM 116:1 TLB

The Discipline of Daily Prayer

Each morning I will look to you in heaven
and lay my requests before you,
praying earnestly.
PSALM 5:3 TLB

*P*rayer does not require special words or high-sounding themes. Prayer is a simple matter of regularly setting aside time to talk to God. A daily prayer habit will help us grow spiritually and draw us into a close and comforting relationship with God. Some people flee from the concept of "routines" or "habits." But these regular activities need not be boring or restrictive. They can be exciting opportunities to interact with the Creator of the universe and influence the world around us.

Our prayer habit can be enhanced by finding a quiet place with a pleasant atmosphere to regularly meet with God. Keeping a Bible, journal, and other helpful books in that special place is also a good idea. If we are faithful to make ourselves available and attentive to God each day, we will reap abundant spiritual dividends.

*L*ord, help me not to let one day go by without spending time talking to You in prayer. Help me make it a habit in my life—one that will bless me and draw me closer to You.

My heart is confident in you, O God;
no wonder I can sing your praises!
Wake up, my soul!

PSALM 108:1 NLT

The Lord Wants to Use Our Talents

And let the beauty of the LORD our God be upon us,
And establish the work of our hands for us;
Yes, establish the work of our hands.

PSALM 90:17 NKJV

*E*ach one of us is absolutely unique and irreplaceable in the eyes of God. And we have each been given talents and abilities that are ours alone. The key to achieving satisfaction and success with our talents is to place them always at the service of God. We should ask for His direction and pray for His guidance so we may use our gifts fruitfully and fully in His eyes. God has a plan for each one of us, and He has equipped us for our journey. Our responsibility is to seek His will and allow Him to perfect and refine our endowments until they are functioning as they were intended. It is then that we can be sure that He will bless the work of our hands.

*L*ord, I give all my talents and abilities to You. I ask You to use me as I grow in my determination to be all that You have created me to be.

The LORD's instruction is right;
it makes our hearts glad.
His commands shine brightly,
and they give us light.

PSALM 19:8 CEV

Faith, Hope, and Love

Yes, Lord, let your constant love surround us,
for our hopes are in you alone.
PSALM 33:22 TLB

Our spiritual strength is founded on the triad of faith, hope, and love. Our Lord shows us how we are to behave with others by actively demonstrating these three virtues through His own

unblemished behavior toward us.

If we take Him at His word, our ordinary, everyday lives should be an acting-out of His promises to us; and our relationships with others should be an energetic, vital mirror image of the trustworthy, loving, and merciful God we have come to know. It is really as simple as one, two, three: faith, hope, love. We must strive for faith, hope, and love if we want to be fully pleasing to God.

Lord, I want to build my life upon the principles of faith, hope, and love. Guide me as I follow Your example, and give me the courage never to waver from that path.

Be of good courage,
And He shall strengthen your heart,
All you who hope in the LORD.

PSALM 31:24 NKJV

Inviting the Lord into Our Homes

My soul shall be satisfied as with marrow and fatness;
and my mouth shall praise thee with joyful lips:
When I remember thee upon my bed.

PSALM 63:5-6 KJV

Home is the center of family life and a reflection of who we are and who we hope to become. Home is where we are fully ourselves. Home is a haven from the world and its distractions, threats, and annoyances. Just as the home is the center of family life, so God should be the center of our homes.

We invite Him into our homes as we look to Him in prayer, personally and as a family group. We invite Him in as we read the Bible and apply its words to our interactions with those nearest and dearest to our hearts. We invite Him in as we fill our homes with symbols of our faith that provide inspiration and comfort. The important thing is for God to be the "Master of our homes" rather than a convenient guest.

Lord, I invite You into my home. I ask You to dwell with us through the good times and the bad. Show us how to live our lives to the fullest through Your indwelling presence.

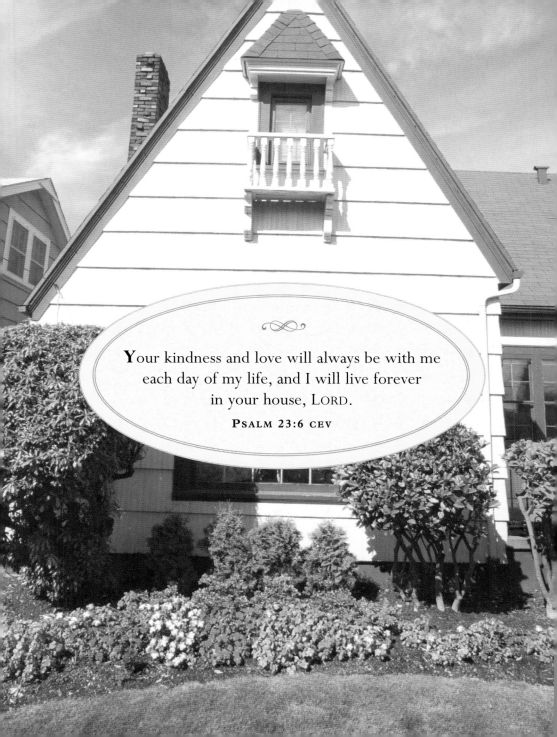

Your kindness and love will always be with me
each day of my life, and I will live forever
in your house, LORD.

PSALM 23:6 CEV

Rewards of Righteous Living

The LORD loves the righteous.

PSALM 146:8 NLT

Righteous living is, quite simply, keeping the letter and the spirit of God's commandments. It is observing His statutes in the form of the Ten Commandments; but it is also going further, and fully embracing the spirit of love that underlies them.

A righteous life is a good life in the eyes of the Lord. A righteous

woman is a woman who trusts in God and lets Him lead her. She molds her behavior according to God's own relationship with His children, as revealed in the Scripture. Kindness, generosity, compassion, and patience are the hallmarks of her daily activities. Confidence and security bless her steps because she knows she walks with God. She is a beacon of divine light in a world too full of darkness. She helps others find their way to Him, the God of all comfort and joy. She is a champion of mercy and justice; she is a peacemaker.

Lord, Your blessings are incomparable. Protect me from all harm and endow my life with the joy that can only come from Your presence.

Cast your burden on the LORD,
and he will sustain you;
he will never permit
the righteous to be moved.

PSALM 55:22 NRSV

God Is in the Details

I will meditate about your glory, splendor, majesty and miracles.

PSALM 145:5 TLB

*I*sn't it marvelous? Just when we need Him most, God surrounds us with reminders of His presence.

He is evident in a tear or in a far-off whistle. He is in the twinkle of a stranger's eye and in a certain shade of blue. He is in the warmth of a handshake and in the missing front teeth of a five-year-old. He is in the hum of the washing machine and in the glow of the Christmas lights. He is between the lines of handwritten letters and in the nervous laughter of teenage girls. He rises up in the aroma of freshly cut grass. He is in the invisible arc made by a hawk on a fine autumn day. He is the energy we use to write our to-do lists, and He is in the itch to take a break in the middle of the day. God is in every sigh, whisper, and exclamation. He is in kept promises and acts of love and mercy.

*L*ord, thank You for Your presence in my life. Fill me with Your goodness and grace, and give me eyes to see the many things You do for me each and every day.

I will thank you, LORD, with all my heart;
I will tell of all the marvelous things you have done.
I will be filled with joy because of you.
I will sing praises to your name, O Most High.

PSALM 9:1-2 NLT

This is the LORD's doing;
it is marvelous in our eyes.
This is the day that the LORD has made;
let us rejoice and be glad in it.

PSALM 118:23-24 NRSV

The Kingdom of God Is Now

Your kingdom is an everlasting kingdom,
and your dominion endures throughout all generations.

PSALM 145:13 NRSV

*H*eaven is usually spoken of as a faraway place that we reach only at the end of a godly life. But we would do well to remember that God's reign over all that He created is right here in the present day, before our eyes and under our noses. And we lack nothing to enter it if we only place our trust in Him and in His commandments.

We don't have to wait for heaven to draw near to the Lord, experience His love, and do His will. Everything we need is available by faith and grace. God has given us the tools to know Him—Scripture, prayer, communities of faithful believers, acts of love, peace, and mercy. All of these pull us toward our true center and spiritual home with God. The foretastes of heaven are abundant if we open our hearts to see them.

*L*ord, open my eyes to see Your goodness and mercy in the midst of this life. Thank You for the love and mercy You pour out on me every day. Thank You for giving me a taste of the good things yet to come.

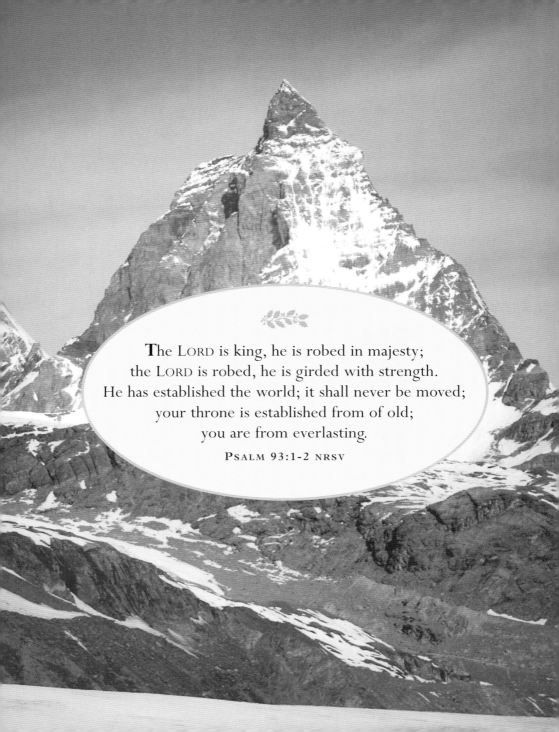

The LORD is king, he is robed in majesty;
the LORD is robed, he is girded with strength.
He has established the world; it shall never be moved;
your throne is established from of old;
you are from everlasting.

PSALM 93:1-2 NRSV

God Brings Out Our Best

May He grant you according to your heart's desire,
And fulfill all your purpose.

PSALM 20:4 NKJV

*M*ost of us remember our parents telling us as little girls, "Always do your best." It's a message we absorb and pass on to our own children as a foundational principle of what it takes to get ahead and be successful in life. At some level, we are always evaluating our performance according to this standard.

But God says that the most certain way to ensure that we are living up to our potential is to place ourselves fully in the care of the Lord.

When we commit our ways and our abilities to Him, we can be sure that He will guide us and help us become all that we can be. We must seek His will in all things, pray for His wisdom and insight into the purpose for our lives, and ask for His help in all we do.

*L*ord, I commit my life to You and ask You to help me fulfill the true purpose for my life. I lay my own attempts to achieve success at Your feet.

Because thou hast been my help,
therefore in the shadow of thy wings will I rejoice.

PSALM 63:7 KJV

Teach me how to live, O LORD.

PSALM 27:11 NLT

God Is Love

The New Testament *reduces the complicated laws of the Old Testament to one overriding rule: Love one another. If we want to know what true love is, we only need to study God's behavior toward us. When we do, we see that He is generous, forbearing, kind, faithful, supportive, nurturing, forgiving, and just. He is everything we want in a Father.*

We exist in God and know God through our own acts of love in the world. He is in the face of everyone we reach out to, no matter from what station in life he or she might come. His love is in our gentle word to a friend in pain, in the simple work making a home for our families, and in the kindness we show to a stranger. When we live in love, we become more and more like our Father.

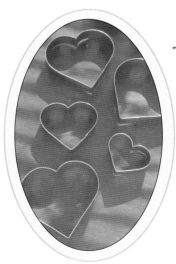

Lord, fill my heart with love for You and for those whose lives I touch each day. Thank You for first loving me and showing me how to love others.

Let your worshipers celebrate
and be glad because of you.

PSALM 70:4 CEV

God's Blessings on Families

And His righteousness to children's children,
To such as keep His covenant.
PSALM 103:17-18 NKJV

By making God the head of our families, we literally put Him in charge as the Defender and Provider. He rewards us with many and varied blessings when we put Him first. Harmony, peace, security,

understanding, kindness, and prosperity flow into our lives in great abundance; and our relationships within and outside our family circle begin to flourish, mature, and become fruitful.

A good way to honor the richness of this gift is by daily joining hands and bowing our heads and praying to God as a family. When we do, everyone feels His strength and grace, for the Lord is with us, confirming and acknowledging our words and intentions. Our relationships are sanctified and blessed by God when we as a family ask Him to care for us and protect us.

Lord, help me to give You Your rightful place of honor in our home. Thank You for Your hand of blessing on our family, bringing us love, joy, and peace.

Your wife will be as fruitful
as a grapevine,
and just as an olive tree
is rich with olives,
your home will be rich
with healthy children.
That is how the LORD will bless
everyone who respects him.

PSALM 128:3-4 CEV

God Reveals Himself in Our Daily Lives

Those who are wise will take all this to heart;
they will see in our history the faithful love of the LORD.

PSALM 107:43 NLT

*A*lthough we sometimes feel that we are alone and He is far away, God is not a distant power. He is an active presence in our everyday lives. When we develop the habit of reading the tone and incidents of our days as if He shaped them, we gain real insight into how to draw closer to Him.

Things don't just "happen." Those things we call "accidents," "surprises," or "discoveries" are really revelations of His love and constant concern for us. We may be puzzled and confused at events for a time, but if we keep our faith and trust in Him, the meaning will be made clear. If we greet each new day with the expectation that the glory, power, and love of the Lord will be revealed in it, our hours will be filled with joy and awe. And His mystery will lead us ever onward toward Him.

*L*ord, help me see Your hand in all the events of my life. I know that even when I feel alone, You are with me, giving my life meaning and purpose.

I remember the days of old,
I think about all your deeds,
I meditate on the works of your hands.

PSALM 143:5 NRSV

God Dispels Confusion and Doubt

Pray to me in time of trouble.
I will rescue you,
and you will honor me.

PSALM 50:15 CEV

We have all experienced the disruption and confusion of moving to a new home, with all our worldly goods packed and transported from the order and familiarity of our old home to the unfamiliar chaos of our new one. We can't find the can opener or the coffee cups, we don't know which box to unpack first, and the ringing phone is buried somewhere behind a chair. It is disorienting and stressful. Our comfortable routines have to be abandoned until we find the things we are looking for, the items necessary to the conduct of our lives. If only we had a map of where everything was packed away!

God has provided a map for our lives. His commandments and teachings give us the meaning and clarity we need to live peacefully and productively. And if we are momentarily confused or doubtful, we can call on Him, and He will help us find what we need to carry on. At those times, and everyone has them, when all meaning seems to have leaked out of our lives, God is right there, waiting for an invitation to step in and set things right.

Lord, when I experience times of confusion and doubt, help me remember that You are there waiting to comfort and guide me.

I waited patiently for the LORD;
and he inclined unto me,
and heard my cry.

PSALM 40:1 KJV

Our Hope Is in God

But happy are those who have the God of Israel as their helper, whose hope is in the LORD their God.

PSALM 146:5 NLT

Hope is a quality we are so accustomed to living with that only in its absence do we truly understand its importance. Hope is what enables us to get out of bed in the morning and get our families off to school and work. Hope is the strength in our backbones that allows us to withstand storms of trouble and pain. Hope keeps us going. Those who lose hope lose the will to live. Our grounds for hope are in God's Word, in the history of steadfast love He has shown toward us, and in the constant care and comfort He gives to all who trust in Him. Our hope is in our reliance on God's blessing and provision for us and the joyous expectation of even greater happiness when we are at last united with Him. Hope puts smiles on our faces as we advance toward the future with patience, courage, confidence, and stability.

Lord, I want to put You first in my life. Keep Your hand on me and don't let me stray from Your will, for You are the Source of my hope.

Let thy mercy, O LORD, be upon us,
according as we hope in thee.

PSALM 33:22 KJV

Making Time for God

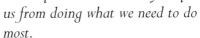

My voice You shall hear in the morning, O LORD;
In the morning I will direct it to You,
And I will look up.
PSALM 5:3 NKJV

We can come up with many excuses for not praying regularly. We are so busy! We go through our days at a dead run and fall into bed at night exhausted. Countless responsibilities and interruptions distract us. There are so many good excuses, but the problem is that they keep

us from doing what we need to do most.

And so, we procrastinate and rationalize. We promise ourselves that we will get started on it tomorrow or tell ourselves that God already knows what we think. (After all, He is God.) And so we try to stave off the anxiety this creates with even more busyness and activity. It's a vicious cycle that often leaves us weak and discouraged. We must do whatever it takes to make an appointment with God and keep it each day!

Lord, help me as I strive to keep my commitment to meet You in prayer every day. I know how much I need that quality time alone with You.

Give heed to the voice of my cry,
My King and my God,
For to You I will pray.

PSALM 5:2 NKJV

Patience as We Wait on the Lord

I wait for the LORD, my soul waits,
and in his word I hope.

PSALM 130:5 NRSV

No one likes to be kept waiting. The hold button on telephones ought to be outlawed, we sometimes think. The line at a popular restaurant, the crowded waiting room of a doctor's office, the plumber who is late, a lunch date who keeps us waiting—these are all time wasters.

But waiting on God is a different matter. We may go through periods during which we feel He isn't listening to our prayers. Though we ardently beseech Him, heaven is silent. During these times, it's important to understand that the "wait" is part of the answer God is giving us. Waiting is part and parcel of the mystery of His plan and the degrees by which it will be unfolded to us. God answers us in His time, not ours.

Lord, help me to cultivate patience, so that I can rest comfortably in the knowledge that You are taking care of all those things that concern me.

Stand in awe, and sin not:
commune with your own heart upon your bed, and be still.
Selah. Offer the sacrifices of righteousness,
and put your trust in the LORD.

PSALM 4:4-5 KJV

Wait for the LORD, and keep to his way,
and he will exalt you to inherit the land.

PSALM 37:34 NRSV

God's Infinite Forgiveness

Order my steps in thy word:
and let not any iniquity have dominion over me.
PSALM 119:133 KJV

*S*ome of us have a hard time apologizing when we are wrong. The simple words "I'm sorry" are loaded with vulnerability and the fear of retribution. And even when we know that forgiveness is forthcoming, it is easy to let pride stand in the way.

Learning to own up to our mistakes is an important step to maturity. This is also true in our relationship with God. But with Him we can be assured that we have nothing to fear and everything to gain, for He has promised to forgive us whenever we come to Him. Because we are God's beloved children, we must apologize when we stray. But we can live our lives in confidence that He wants to—and will—forgive us when we come to him contritely.

*L*ord, forgive me when I let fear and pride come between us. I lay my life before You now and ask You to cleanse me and make me pleasing in Your sight.

For I know my transgressions,
and my sin is ever before me.
Against you, you alone, have I sinned,
and done what is evil in your sight,
so that you are justified in your sentence
and blameless when you pass judgment.

PSALM 51:3-4 NRSV

The Gift of Giving

He is ever merciful, and lends;
And his descendants are blessed.

PSALM 37:26 NKJV

*G*iving generously from the heart is extremely satisfying for many reasons, but the most important reason is that it glorifies God. When we give freely, we are acknowledging the abundant, unreserved generosity He has poured out on us, His children.

We should also remember that there are many ways to give. Money is often the first thing that comes to mind, but today with our busy, even frantic, schedules, the gift of time is often an even greater sacrifice. No matter how we choose to give, we can always be sure that God is truly pleased and anxious to pour out His grace on us in return.

*L*ord, open my heart and open my hands to share all You have given me. Thank You for pouring out Your blessings on my life.

For you are the Fountain of life;
our light is from your Light.
Pour out your unfailing love on those who know you!
Never stop giving your salvation
to those who long to do your will.

PSALM 36:9-10 TLB

Grace Sufficient for the Hour

The LORD is gracious and full of compassion,
Slow to anger and great in mercy.
The LORD is good to all,
And His tender mercies are over all His works.

PSALM 145:8-9 NKJV

*G*race is God's unmerited favor, His undeserved mercy, His boundless compassion. This wondrous gift comes to us because we are fortunate enough to be His children. And because we are His, He loves us unconditionally.

Grace is our birthright as children of God. We fully avail ourselves of this bounty by placing our complete trust in Him. We have access to His grace by having confidence in His promises. When we act on this confidence in our Heavenly Father, we find that nothing is too great a challenge, no obstacle too large to overcome. Though we may approach a tough situation with trepidation, knowing the limitations of our own meager abilities, we can ask for His help and be certain that He will give it.

*L*ord, help me open my eyes to the heritage You have given me as Your child. Thank You especially for protecting and supporting me at all times.

You are merciful, LORD!
You are kind and patient
and always loving.
You are good to everyone,
and you take care
of all your creation.

PSALM 145:8-9 CEV

Making a Sanctuary for the Spirit

Our God, here in your temple
we think about your love.
PSALM 48:9 CEV

*M*any women find that designating a specific time and creating a particular place to meet with God helps them bring more focus and consistency to their quiet time. It is good advice. Some women like to set aside time in the morning. But the truth is that just about any time of the day or night will work just fine, as long as it is explicitly reserved for this specific purpose and becomes part of a daily routine. Where we meet with God each day is also a matter of personal choice. It can be anywhere, inside or outside, as long as it is quiet, peaceful, and conducive to reflection and meditation.

Although we pray throughout the day, and even are instructed to pray "constantly," having a little retreat from the world's cares and "buzz" is a great boost for our prayer lives. Here, we can bring our hearts, minds, and souls fully to God.

*L*ord, thank You for meeting me here in our special place. I hope to make it a place of worship, a place where I can leave the world behind as I bask in the wonder of Your love for me.

As the deer pants for streams of water,
so I long for you, O God.
I thirst for God, the living God.
When can I come and stand before him?

PSALM 42:1-2 NLT

The Lord Renews and Refreshes Our Lives

For with You is the fountain of life;
In Your light we see light.

PSALM 36:9 NKJV

*J*ust as this Scripture says, God is the fountain of life. He is the Source of all good things, and we must go to Him for nurturing and encouragement, day after day. Our regeneration in God is a lifelong affair.

God is the light by which we see the world and ourselves and understand our reason for being. Were it not for Him, we would not exist, let alone have eyes to see. He discloses to us the drama of all that He has created. If we stray too far from His light, we grow dim and the world is plunged into darkness. Throughout our lives, we must stay close to Him in order to fulfill the purpose for which we were created.

*L*ord, help me stay close to You, returning day after day to be strengthened and refreshed by Your love and care. I want to be a reflection of Your light in the world around me.

I will never forget thy precepts:
for with them thou hast quickened me.

PSALM 119:93 KJV

Wash me thoroughly from my iniquity,
And cleanse me from my sin.

PSALM 51:2 NKJV

All Creation Praises Him

*All creation, come praise
the name of the LORD.
Praise his name alone.*

PSALM 148:13 CEV

In the fullness of summer, in all of its green lushness, we can sometimes hear a noisy symphony of natural sounds. Crickets, frogs, cicadas, birds, dogs, and cows all contribute to the song of praise to God the Creator. How can they keep from singing?

The other seasons have their own harmonies and melodies of praise. In autumn we can hear the owl at night and the crow in the morning raise their voices to mingle with the crisp breezes; deer, rabbits, raccoons, and other game rustle in the dry foliage. Winter's icy silence and keening winds make their own distinct frosty music, slow and majestic, a background to our celebration of the Savior's birth. Then spring, on the rebound from winter's solemnity, sings in full throat with the bustling silliness of a schoolyard at recess, bursting with energy and ready to get on with life once more. The first choirs the world ever heard are still in place, still singing. Praise is a natural activity that issues from a God-filled life.

Lord, my heart is filled with praise and my lips with thanksgiving. I am in awe of Your creation. Thank You for Your tender care over all that You have made.

O LORD my God, thou art very great;
thou art clothed with honour and majesty.
Who coverest thyself with light as with a garment:
who stretchest out the heavens like a curtain.

PSALM 104:1-2 KJV

Prayer in a Dry Season

Why am I discouraged?
Why so sad?
I will put my hope in God!
PSALM 43:5 NLT

*E*very woman has spiritual dry spells, no matter how devout she may be or how deep her faith. These times can be precipitated by the loss of a loved one, a personal defeat, or any number of adverse circumstances. During these uncomfortable, barren times, it often

becomes difficult to pray. God may seem like a vague idea rather than a living reality.

It is comforting to bear in mind that this is not an unusual occurrence. Many of the heroes of the faith have experienced the same loss of direction and have had their faith tested. Even the psalmist David suffered notorious depressions brought on by treachery, betrayal, adversaries, and his own sins. The important thing is not to give up. Even though we feel as if we are only going through the motions, we must persist in prayer. Faith and vitality will return. God does not forsake us.

*L*ord, I know there will be times when my faith is tested and I cannot feel You as near as I do right now. When those times come, I will depend upon Your promise that You will never leave me nor forsake me.

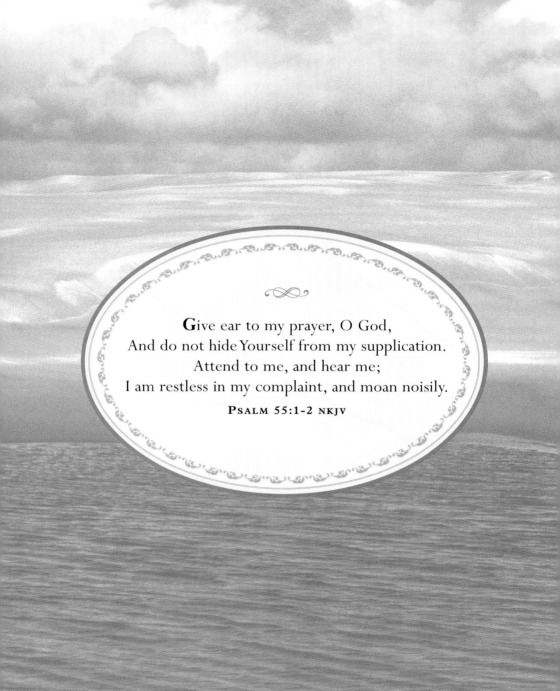

Give ear to my prayer, O God,
And do not hide Yourself from my supplication.
Attend to me, and hear me;
I am restless in my complaint, and moan noisily.

PSALM 55:1-2 NKJV

Honor God by Ministering to His People

He will deliver the needy when he cries,
The poor also, and him who has no helper.
PSALM 72:12 NKJV

When we put our lives in God's hands and commit to do His will, He uses us mightily to bring comfort and peace to other people. By helping others, we act as conduits for God's love in the world.

There is meaning and intention behind every circumstance we face. Oftentimes, it only becomes clear in hindsight. The depressed neighbor, the neglected children of a friend, the harried checkout person at the grocery store, and the irritable plumber who comes to fix the sink all need our lovingkindness and reassurance. These people are precious to God and should be to us as well. We can use each new day as an opportunity to do God's work in the world, work that brings love and peace into the lives of everyone we encounter.

Lord, let me be an instrument of Your love to all those around me. Fill my mouth with words that will encourage and strengthen. Thank You for letting me share Your light with others.

My help comes from the LORD,
who made heaven and earth.

PSALM 121:2 NRSV

The Divine Mystery at the Heart of Life

Such knowledge is too wonderful for me,
too great for me to know!

PSALM 139:6 NLT

*G*od's power and love are too great for us to fully comprehend in this life. Great art, poetry, and music perhaps best convey His awesome

majesty. When we pause from our daily routine, struck by the intensity of a sunset or the beauty of a child, we catch a glimpse of the divine mystery at the heart of life. And it only whets our appetite for more. It is a glimmer of God's handiwork, vanishing as quickly as it has captured our attention.

The attitude of awe is a powerful reminder of our littleness and God's greatness, and it is our proper posture toward God and His miraculous creation. Let us reacquire the receptive mind of the child so that we may never lose the "wow" we feel for the stunning beauty of God's grandeur in the world.

*L*ord, give me the heart of a child, a heart that is constantly amazed and awed by Your greatness.

O give thanks to the Lord of lords,
for his steadfast love endures forever;
who alone does great wonders,
for his steadfast love endures forever.

PSALM 136:3-4 NRSV

Claiming God's Blessings

He fills my life with good things.

PSALM 103.5:5 NLT

*G*od's blessings are available to all who put their trust in Him and keep His commandments. The beauty and simplicity of His abundance are so obvious they are sometimes hard to see. His promises are everywhere in Scripture. He will be our Father if we will be His children; if we honor and obey Him, He will withhold nothing from us. All we have to do is ask.

He forgives our trespasses and provides righteousness and justice

when we are treated unfairly; He is merciful and gracious; He is slow to get angry and full of unfailing love. Sin and despair are the only obstacles between us and God's many blessings. They cloud our vision and prevent us from seeing things as they are. As the psalm says, "He understands how weak we are; he knows we are only dust" (Psalm 103:14 NLT), and so He is eternally patient with us and sends us the grace we need to overcome our weaknesses.

*L*ord, thank You for the blessings You have placed in my life. Cleanse my heart that I might receive all You have provided for me.

See for yourself the way his mercies
shower down on all who trust in him.
If you belong to the Lord, reverence him;
for everyone who does this has everything he needs.

PSALM 34:8-9 TLB

God's Love Makes Us Wealthy

*See the one who would not take
refuge in God,
but trusted in abundant riches,
and sought refuge in wealth!*

PSALM 52:7 NRSV

*A*s a society, we are constantly bombarded with the message that
we should want more, buy more, have more. Doing so will bring us
happiness, we are told. Our minds are assaulted with this "gospel" every

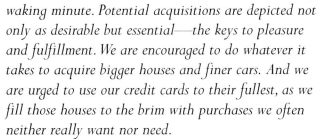

waking minute. Potential acquisitions are depicted not
only as desirable but essential—the keys to pleasure
and fulfillment. We are encouraged to do whatever it
takes to acquire bigger houses and finer cars. And we
are urged to use our credit cards to their fullest, as we
fill those houses to the brim with purchases we often
neither really want nor need.

And the saddest thing is that ultimately "things"
can never really satisfy us. As soon as we have acquired
a certain possession, the novelty begins to wear off, and
we begin to yearn for something else. We must live a
life in which God is the center. His love is the wealth
we truly want, and only in Him will we find peace.

*L*ord, help me remember that "things" cannot satisfy the deep longing
in my heart that can only be filled by You. I know that I am truly
wealthy because You are in my life.

We are merely moving shadows,
and all our busy rushing ends in nothing.
We heap up wealth for someone else to spend.

PSALM 39:6 NLT

Accepting the Lord's Guidance

The LORD says,
"I will make you wise and show you where to go.
I will guide you and watch over you."

PSALM 32:8 NCV

*W*hen we are close to God, regularly praying, studying the Scriptures, and seeking His counsel, we are primed for and attuned to the guidance He is offering for our lives. As we are paying attention to Him, we notice that He is paying attention to us.

Our thoughts and feelings are honed to pick up His direction and advice for our everyday activities as well as our major decisions and challenges. The Holy Spirit whispers to us throughout the day, inspiring us to choose wisely and behave properly. Our own spirits are at peace, and we receive blessings in our work and families.

*L*ord, I look to You for direction and counsel as I make important decisions in my life. I ask You to give me a listening ear to hear Your voice and a heart that is quick to obey.

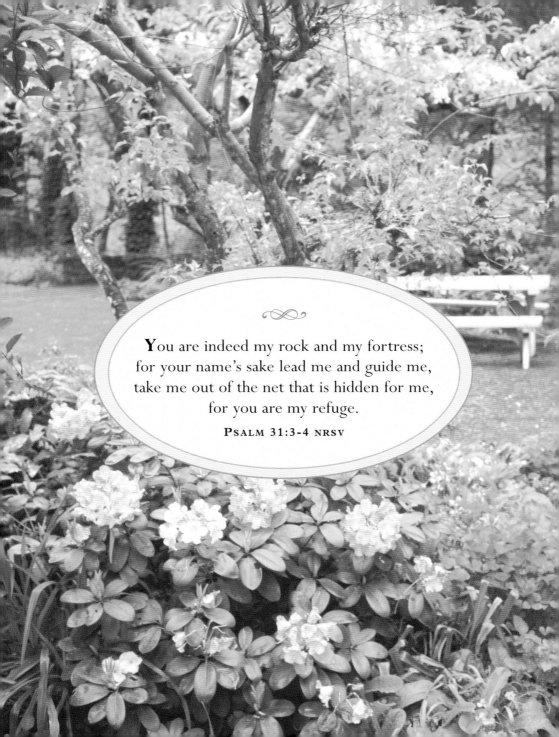

You are indeed my rock and my fortress;
for your name's sake lead me and guide me,
take me out of the net that is hidden for me,
for you are my refuge.

PSALM 31:3-4 NRSV

Finding Our Lives in God

O taste and see that the LORD is good:
blessed is the man that trusteth in him.

PSALM 34:8 KJV

*T*he central questions in life—Who am I? What am I? Why was I born?—are troubling until we find the answers that ring true for us. These questions can be difficult for those who have no foundation in faith. Being human, we require meaning in our lives; and if we do not find it, we are sometimes tempted to feel that life is not worth the effort.

We can only find the answers to these questions as we grow in our relationship with God. For it is He who made us and it is He who holds the key to our lives. As we get to know Him better, He reveals to us the purpose for which we were created. We discover that we are His children and heirs to all His love and grace and mercy.

*L*ord, thank You for creating me and giving my life meaning and purpose. Your love makes all the difference.

He has put a new song in my mouth—
Praise to our God.

PSALM 40:3 NKJV

God's Face in the Stranger at the Door

For I am your passing guest,
an alien, like all my forebears.

PSALM 39:12 NRSV

We've all had it happen before: the knock at the door at an odd hour. Someone rather shabby we've never seen before is facing us through the glass. Our first instinct is usually to shut the door quickly. We've read the stories in the newspapers . . . home invaders . . . thieves . . . and worse. We can't be too careful, given the "way things are today." We tell our kids not to talk to "strangers"; we avoid the disheveled man on the city street corner with the cup in his hand; we step around the homeless person sleeping on the sidewalk.

Scripture urges us to show goodwill to foreigners and those less fortunate. We are to love them and relieve their distress whenever we are able. Scripture says that when we show mercy and kindness to one who is downtrodden, we are showing kindness and mercy to Christ.

Lord, in an effort to protect myself, I sometimes neglect those in need. Open my heart to show kindness, my eyes to see opportunities, and my hands to give comfort and solace whenever I can.

For he delivers the needy when they call,
the poor and those who have no helper.

PSALM 72:12 NRSV

Soul Food

*I will meditate on the glorious splendor of Your majesty,
And on Your wondrous works.*

PSALM 145:5 NKJV

*W*hen you walk through the door to your office every morning,
how do you feel? Is your desk or work area warm and inviting? The
workplace is where we spend a large part of our lives, and it should be
as conducive to peaceful, productive work as possible. Divorcing our

personal lives from our jobs makes
creating a happy atmosphere
difficult. Instead, we should keep in
mind what is truly important to us
by integrating symbols of our "real"
life into our work environment.
Photos, mementos, and other objects
of personal significance warm the
atmosphere and inspire a creative,
enthusiastic approach to
responsibilities. They also help us
keep things in perspective and
remind us who we are working for.
These little treasures are like soul
food because they feed us emotionally and spiritually and lead our
hearts back to God, the center of our lives.

*L*ord, bless my work area with peace. And help me carry out my job
responsibilities with diligence and excellence.

I have calmed and quieted my soul,
like a weaned child with its mother;
my soul is like the weaned child that is with me.

PSALM 131:2 NRSV

But it is good for me to draw near to God:
I have put my trust in the Lord GOD,
that I may declare all thy works.

PSALM 73:28 KJV

The Value of Tradition
and Ritual

*They shall abundantly utter the memory of thy great goodness,
and shall sing of thy righteousness.*

PSALM 145:7 KJV

*W*e honor and commemorate our Christian heritage by observing
little traditions and rituals that are special to us and to our families.
They are reminders of a past shared and a future anticipated in the
steadfast love of God.

From time-honored holiday traditions
to small daily rituals, such as
grace before meals and prayers
and stories before bedtime,
these observances reaffirm
our relationships with each
other and with God. They
cause us to pause and
reflect upon those things
that give our lives meaning.
As we draw together with
friends and family members on
these occasions, our love for one
another is refreshed and our spirits
are lifted.

*L*ord, thank You for giving us reason to celebrate. You are truly the
God of all hope. You bring happiness and fulfillment to our lives.

All the ends of the world
Shall remember and turn to the LORD,
And all the families of the nations
Shall worship before You.

PSALM 22:27 NKJV

Believe in Miracles

For the Lord has done this wonderful miracle for me. . . .
I shall live! Yes, in his presence — here on earth!

PSALM 116:7,9 TLB

$\mathcal{M}$iracles happen every day. Some are extraordinary acts of God that alter the natural course of events, and some consist of situations where individuals have overcome tremendous odds to achieve their goals. But no matter how we define them, miracles do happen. For those who have the courage to believe, no situation is so dire, no goal so remote that we cannot expect God's help and intervention on our behalf.

Miracles are unexplainable, but so are the other aspects of our relationship with God. We don't know why God loves us unconditionally and completely, but He does. We don't know why He listens to and answers our prayers, but He does. We don't know how miracles happen any more than we know how God created us in the first place. But we don't have to understand (indeed, we are incapable of understanding); we only have to believe.

Lord, thank You for the miracles You have brought to my life. As I look around me, I see all that You have done and I am humbled by Your goodness to me.

Our fathers trusted in You;
They trusted, and You delivered them.
They cried to You, and were delivered;
They trusted in You, and were not ashamed.

PSALM **22:4-5** NKJV

Then they cried to the Lord in their troubles,
and he helped them and delivered them.
He spoke, and they were healed—
snatched from the door of death.

PSALM **107:19-20** TLB

People Are to Be Helped, Not Shunned

Good and upright is the LORD;
Therefore He teaches sinners in the way.
PSALM 25:8 NKJV

*W*hen we were children, our parents warned us to stay away from "bad" companions who might cause us to stray from the right path and participate in activities that were harmful to us and others. Certainly

this was and is good advice for the very young and the easily influenced.

But we learn from Scripture that God loves all His children and wants all of us to be united with Him. We also learn that as believers we have a responsibility to be a blessing not only to those who are living godly lives but also to those who are not. We are mirrors of God's love in the world; we must reflect and pass along the goodness and mercy shown to us. And we are able to actively practice this commandment most notably when we reach out to people who do not know that God loves them and has a wonderful purpose for their lives.

*L*ord, give me the courage to reach out to those who do not yet know You. Give me the words to speak truth and love into their lives.

For Your name's sake, O Lord,
Pardon my iniquity, for it is great.

Psalm 25:11 nkjv

Who can understand his errors?
Cleanse me from secret faults.
Keep back Your servant also from presumptuous sins;
Let them not have dominion over me.

Psalm 19:12-13 nkjv

The Healing Power of God

*P*rayer is good medicine. It's a fact, and medical science has finally caught on. Studies show that individuals who pray regularly and commit their welfare to the Lord recover from serious illnesses and traumas faster than those who have no faith in God. Our outlook on

life is more positive, our hope for the future stronger. And as far as minor illnesses are concerned, we even get fewer colds than those who face life without the advantage of genuine faith.

Prayer and thanksgiving relieve stress, alleviate anxiety, promote positive thinking, and generally foster happiness and contentment. Is it any wonder that such things contribute to our health? When we know that God is in charge of everything and is our guide, we are far less likely to take ourselves too seriously.

*L*ord, faith is so important to every aspect of my life. Without it, I would be lonely and without hope. Thank You for being there to hear me when I pray.

Come, O Lord, and make me well.
In your kindness save me.

PSALM 6:4 TLB

Now I know that the LORD saves His anointed;
He will answer him from His holy heaven
With the saving strength of His right hand.

PSALM 20:6 NKJV

Shh, Listen

O rider in the heavens, the ancient heavens;
listen, he sends out his voice, his mighty voice.

PSALM 68:33 NRSV

*O*f the five senses given to us, listening is the one most poorly used. And yet it is the key to real communication with others. Often when we ask questions, we have already formulated the answers we expect. When we engage in conversation or listen to music, we often have preconceived ideas of what we are going to hear. Conditioned by habit or limited thinking, our expectations drown out what is new and interesting. We are prisoners of our past experiences and deaf to what is vital and "telling" in the world.

If we are to respond with our "best self" to the world God presents to us, we must dust off those old eardrums and turn up the volume. We have to pay attention to the pauses between words, the sighs, the tone of voice coming our way. We have to let the sounds of life—the birdsongs, the car horns, the whistling teakettles—get through to us.

*L*ord, open my ears to hear the sounds around me—the sounds that wake me to the beauty and grandeur of Your wonderful world.

They speak without a sound or a word;
their voice is silent in the skies;
yet their message has gone out to all the earth,
and their words to all the world.

PSALM 19:3-4 NLT

Come, O children, listen to me;
I will teach you the fear of the LORD.

PSALM 34:11 NRSV

Yielding Our Spirits to God

Thy testimonies also are my delight.

PSALM 119:24 KJV

*S*ome of our thorniest ethical quandaries occur at work. Office politics, power plays, and gossip, as well as on-the-job pressures, often bring out the worst in people. Because livelihood and financial security are involved, the stakes are high, and people go to extremes to get the upper hand or come out on top.

But we must remember that we don't check our values and principles at the door when we go to work. Our values make us who we are, children of God intent on abiding in His will at all times. His precepts are written in our hearts. They are the flawless and unerring guide for our behavior. No unexpected circumstance is exempt from them. No challenge at work can overcome them. With them, we are perfectly outfitted to deal in a just and merciful manner with everything that comes our way.

*L*ord, in Your love and mercy, You have given me all I need to succeed in my life, including my job. Help me to deal in love with those who wrong me.

What a glorious Lord!
He who daily bears our burdens
also gives us our salvation.

PSALM 68:19 TLB

At Peace with the World in God

He makes me to lie down in green pastures;
He leads me beside the still waters.
He restores my soul.

PSALM 23:2-3 NKJV

Trying to live without God is unimaginably self-defeating. We are vulnerable to every sting, swipe, and bludgeon that comes our way. Despite all the intelligence and cunning we have been gifted with by Him, if we do not rest in Him and place all our hope in Him, we really don't have a "prayer" of succeeding at anything we do.

Without Him, demons of self-doubt goad us and undermine our best efforts. We are eaten alive by anxiety and become easy prey for despair and defeat. We abide in the world in fear and trembling. But with Him, we are safe and secure! We are swathed in a glow of love and peace. We are able to become all He intended us to be.

Lord, thank You for giving me victory over the world through my relationship with You. No longer will I be victimized by my own weaknesses, for when I am weak, You are strong.

I will lie down in peace and sleep,
for though I am alone, O Lord,
you will keep me safe.

PSALM 4:8 TLB

Only God gives inward peace,
and I depend on him.

PSALM 62:5 CEV

The Forgiving Heart

Look on my affliction and my pain,
And forgive all my sins.

PSALM 25:18 NKJV

At some time during our lives, we all experience the painful betrayal of a friend and the hurt and disappointment that goes with it. When this happens, it is natural to feel a wave of anger rising up in our hearts. We may even find ourselves wanting revenge. Nothing about

this type of experience is comfortable. It leaves us feeling restless, agitated, smarting, tense with the almost physical compulsion to deliver a counter-blow.

When these instances occur, let us remember to take a deep breath and let it all go. Yes, let it go! Just as our Lord has countless times forgiven us for our own bad behavior toward Him, He will help to heal the hurt and sweep the anger out of our hearts.

*L*ord, when friends turn against me and my heart aches from the sting of betrayal, let my thoughts be of Your grace and forgiveness. Let me give to others what You have given me.

Oh, what joy for those
whose rebellion is forgiven,
whose sin is put out of sight!

PSALM 32:1 NLT

God's Tender Mercies

The LORD is good to all:
and his tender mercies are over all his works.

PSALM 145:9 KJV

No one knows us like God; every secret wish, shameful weakness, latent talent, or buried pain is plainly displayed before Him. He loves us in the fullness of who we are, forgiving us of every sin, protecting us from every adversity. He is there like a mother to pick us up, dust us off, and kiss away our wounds. He is there like a father to guard and protect us and to hug us in His strong arms.

His mercies are mighty in effectiveness and breathtaking in precision. His mercies are startlingly accurate and give us exactly what we need when we need it.

For example, we may think we need more money; He may know that what we really need is to reorient our priorities. We may be disappointed because we didn't get a job or we missed an opportunity; He may know that what we think we need is not in our best interest. If we let Him, He salves all our hurts in an intimate, knowing, and kind way.

Lord, You know me so well, better than I know myself. And You know what is best for me. I place myself in Your care and thank You for Your tender love that brings me all that You know I need.

Hear me, O LORD,
for Your lovingkindness is good;
Turn to me according to the multitude
of Your tender mercies.

PSALM 69:16 NKJV

A Time for Rest

With all my heart,
I will celebrate,
and I can safely rest.
PSALM 16:9 CEV

Rest is not just sleep or sedentary inactivity; it is also loafing, goofing off, hanging out, wandering around, sauntering, and killing time. Rest is that restorative and unfocused piddling time where we play, leaving obligations and responsibilities on our desks for a while. We just let things happen; we don't try to make things happen. We go for undirected walks in our imaginations where we are like small children, ready for the next adventure to turn up. For a while we let go of our cares and skip along behind Him, our Father, curious and relaxed, in a little Eden of time. Who knows what will happen? We have "taken off" the ordinary and are wearing a different pair of spectacles that let us see things with new eyes. We're like butterflies on a summer morning. Doing nothing is an important part of life that revives waning spirits, and we "do nothing" best in the security and comfort of God's love.

Lord, teach me to let myself rest in Your love and care, releasing every burden to You. Thank You for restoring and refreshing me as I place my trust in You.

You let me rest in fields
of green grass.
You lead me to streams
of peaceful water,
and you refresh my life.

PSALM 23:2 CEV

Joy

Heart, body, and soul are filled with joy. . . .
You have let me experience the joys of life
and the exquisite pleasures of your own eternal presence.
PSALM 16:9,11 TLB

Joy is the gift of a good God. It beats ice cream, the best movie, mountain climbing, sky diving, the Super Bowl, a hole-in-one, an Oscar. Joyful people whistle, sing, dance, clap, smile, laugh, hoot, holler, turn flips, hop up and down, turn somersaults, and fly through the air in their dreams like Superman.

Joyful people are people on the move; arms and legs, hearts and souls, whirling, they rip through the world repeating everywhere what they've heard. Joy is the jubilant chorus all living things make singing the praises of God. Joy is the thank-you, thank-you, thank-you from the bottom of our hearts that erupts when we are put in touch with what really matters. Joy is the irrepressible buoyancy we feel when we have been forgiven.

*L*ord, thank You for filling my heart and life with joy.

I will be glad, yes, filled with joy because of you.
I will sing your praises, O Lord God.

PSALM 9:2 TLB

Heaven

And when I awake in heaven,
I will be fully satisfied,
for I will see you face to face.

PSALM 17:15 TLB

*W*e use the word "heaven" to refer to the joyous fulfillment of the purpose of our lives—union with God. Certainly life offers us many fleeting foretastes of heaven (which we happily call "heavenly"), yet our present lives are truly only preparation for the ultimate reward God has for us. All the pain, care, and imperfections of life will fall away. The restless yearning that goads and prods us will be gone at last. We will finally become whole in the Father, who is love. We and our loved ones—family members, friends, heroes—will be permanently reunited. All our errors will be forgiven. All distance between us and love will be erased.

We will have perfect rest and happiness and complete freedom from want and anxiety. The ache at the center of our being will be filled with the perfect comfort of divine love. Let heaven keep us going as we allow God's unbreakable promise to lead us through this life to the joy that is in Him.

*L*ord, thank You for heaven and all that it holds for me and for those I love. And thank You for sending Your Holy Spirit to indwell me so that I may taste of heaven here on earth.

Praise him, ye heavens of heavens,
and ye waters that be above the heavens.
Let them praise the name of the LORD:
for he commanded, and they were created.

PSALM 148:4-5 KJV

This and other books in the Psalms Gift Edition™ series are available from your local bookstore.

Lighthouse Psalms
Garden Psalms
Love Psalms
Friendship Psalms
Psalms for Women

If you have enjoyed this book, or if it has impacted your life, we would like to hear from you.
Please contact us at:

Honor Books
Department E
P.O. Box 55388
Tulsa, Oklahoma 74155